one's own
bubble
philosophical poem

mhao knee

Imprint

One´s Own Bubble   Philosophical Poem
Text: Mhao Knee
Graphics : Mhao Knee
ISBN: 9789403609799

Copyright 2020
The work, including all its parts, is protected by copyright.
Any use without the consent of the author is not permitted.

Cover_Photography: Maria Koehne, https://v-arts.net
Published by k_editor / via bookmundo.
Maria Koehne / Schlesische Strasse 31 / D-10997 Berlin

Printed in Germany.

The Deutsche Nationalbibliothek / German National Library lists
this publication in the German National Bibliography.

one´s own bubble

philosophical poem

human being

is part of nature

not out of nature

a path to go

working out good thoughts
applying yourself to good actions

have you been successful ?

a reached limit ?

beyond that limit
 go beyond

the perfect action is

going

to be

born

the way you surrender,

it just happens

when you recognize

what is

then you are

here

acknowledgement absorbs

the whole universe

It is

make the step

of

acknowledgement

that it is

It is

what

happens

to you

anchoring yourself

not from a bad side

no devotion

all that service

be loved

just loved

limitless

unlimited

there is no knowledge

of the self

at the end of the way

as human being

end is impossible

I am not the door

that **faces** a great gift

you are the **light**

choose who you are

be with you

play

nobody argues with you

the whole dream a dream

unreal thoughts

each kind of defense unreal

I am is real

It is. I am.

before the world is

I am

eternal life

it is

nothing very rich

for your intellect

it is

simply a

childs stage

act

good times

good thoughts

you want me to study

I will not ...

what she does ... what he does ...

oh oh oh ...

don´t react

there was a piece

that exploded

act

from

that

I am

only the **infinite**

is in knowing

g o o d actions,

not the intellect

is there any

perfect action ?

never act by yourself

b e

a c t

ego is part of what is

murder is part of

nature

rape is part of nature

man is not outside of nature

there is

no free will

for humans
being part
of nature

be

and want to be

free

from nature

going

b a c k

h o m e

consider what do you want

you want ease

it keeps you as a person
somewhere

like .. I am going to kill that guy
because
I don´t want to die ...

and
you don´t want
the fullness.

i t   i s   n o t.

it is very simple

you are that
fullness

stay with the
real beyond

work out the human being

being at ease

being in meditation

good talks

bad talks

making it possible

knowing yourself.

i t   i s

.

you are that

f u l l n e s s

act

from that stage

the only thing that works in life

is

being

yourself

surrender does

not

come from a

concept

in which you do

believe

when you

don´t believe

whatever

you believe

        you can say

        you believe it

        you can say

        you don´t believe

what is in the here and now

beyond two thoughts

the

white cow

she laps up

the milk of the hand

wishing some fruit

fresh fruits

for her

and her sisters

a higher

frequency layer

the way

of the voice

c h a n g e s

w h e r e v e r

you are   from here

you respond

space

is something bending

space creates gravity

and the mars

the earth

particles

of matter

you look at it

it disappears

it comes back

it disappears

the answer is not outside

as soon as you look at something

as soon it is gone

that peace

in the principle that

is before the big bang

that is It

before

space and time

less important

by time

out of interpolarity

coming out of eternity

extraordinary powerful

it makes all ideas

of you melt away

the same

point before

creation

stillness speaks to stillness

you speak to yourself

I am I

I am

staying within the point

before **creation**

still

you are stillness

forget about

the poor god

out of concept

of the human

mind

                                                  god
                                           of the
                                    theologicans

s u r r e n d e r to that I a m

I am That

experience

do not act

you are not   your experience

you are sitting

in the point before creation

at the bank of the Ganges

the expression of I is diversity

the juice of I Am is reality

stillness

is still there

s t a y

the whole day
don´t care about your thoughts
the mind itself is like a monkey

f o c u s

accepting only
the r e a l as real

stop feeling guilty
forget guilt
stay with stillness

I
belong
to stillness

stay in stillness

d e p t h of infinite

whatever the way they act
whatever the way they seem to be
just what happens
whatever the way they are

It is I

It is

l o v e

we have our limits
as human beings
with human territories
and attractions

missing

s t i l l n e s s

we are not in charge
of madmen

if there is an opportunity
to fight

from out of the point of stillness erases

the c o u r a g e

the ego speaks
what is wrong in the world

what do people do
when a man is beaten
in front of the bus

It
is
n o t h i n g

defend your

own life

go to high regions

by acting from stillness

be successful

i n   t h e   a c t

if you speak from stillness

thoughts will crumble into

little chips soaked in water

be surprised

that It is what It is

get conviction

of b e i n g stillness

everywhere is your family

everywhere is your home

when there is I

there is love

b e y o n d   t i m e

love is also

I

internal being

that is me

that is you

you are at home

finally

all that is to do

is anchoring

find the source

of everything

                                    the wave

                       is sitting in stillness

                                 engaging

                         the depth of water

                                    be free

                                 recognize

                                   the goal

                       whatever experience

                              others have

                       which is not yours

                           talk about yours

                                theres is just

a poor little guy

knowing high

without opinion

to hold anyone

if it is not a stage of experience

it is an opinion

what is past is past

what is future is future

w h a t   i s ,   i s

everything is It

everything is

reality is

in the here and now

there is a history of individual

and a history of individuals

like a nation

it is the same thing

don´t be into the bubble

of the dream

of anyone

s t a y i n y o u r

o w n b u b b l e

only for the sake
of the truth

the truth
that we call

i t   i s

stay
in your own
b u b b l e s

everybody
has one
b u b b l e

history is the history
of humanity
it is still building
everyday

stay in your own bubble

I am includes

the history of
the dinosaurs
the history of
the big bang
and the history
before the big bang

there is no space
and time

I am It

you stand still

I am That

that stillness

the history
of the human beings
is limited
change of mind
change of history

the mind

is limited

        it is not all inclusive

        no private history

        at the end of the day

        there is no history

        all history is

a p p e a r a n c e

i n   t h e   I

the

infinite

includes

history

billions of years before

billions of years after

we are creating

a subjective history

by believing in

an objective history

I am

includes

every history

it is easier

for a camel

to pass the hole

of a needle

than for a rich man

to realize

the real

if powers are needed

                    to manifest

          it comes if it is needed

                      earth

in his mouth

                the earth

                the planets

                the universe

                the universes

b i l l i o n s

o f   u n i v e r s e s

b i l l i o n s

o f   y e a r s

b i l l i o n s

of

t i m e

                from there back to

                the little form

the I a m   in you

is the ocean

manifesting

as a wave

take the form of
one of the watches
established in the
infinite

unmovable

unexpressable

unreachable

He is That
I am That
and I am not
the personal error
that I have done

forgiveness

you are worthy

children of the divine

responsible for the acts
you have done
when you have taken
a turn in your life
going back home

your sins
are forgiven

forgivenness is

about having nothing to do

just acknowledging

an act of recognition

g o

t h r o u g h

reality

starts in the state

in which you are

n o w

the now

is a cow

that brings

me back home

in the field of

the almighty

forget the past

move forward

when someone

comes and hurts

do not react

n o   r e a c t

don´t serve emotion

the manifestation is here

as a mirror

I Am is the first

manifestation

you are given

before I Am

you dream

the deep sleep stage

a light of you

you are the light

understand

the real you

beyond words

I am stands before time

I am creates

space and

time

we are here

before creation

in that point before creation

I am is absorbed in a

deep sleep stage

the stage

in which you are now as it is

n o w is the change

I am forgiven
I do not have to care
about the evil that
I have done

don´t be disturbed

in I a m

it will bring
enlightenment

e n l i g h t e n m e n t

is just a word
don´t be attracted

what you judge

is what

y o u a r e

there is a perfect

justice in the world

trust

you have a choice

to judge the world

or to say

i t i s

p e r f e c t

act in the

world with wisdom

find what compassion is

perfect for learning

perfect for being what I am

intellects want to judge

act from a different state

not from the ego state

do not judge

look at the suffering

human beings are causing

is there a perfection

about it ?

a good reason ?

a

h u m a n   h e a r t

is harder than stone

at the beginning

there is an

e v o l u t i o n

we are part of nature

we are not the centre

of the universe

we have such a sense

of importance

we are not that important

s u r r e n d e r

d o n o t j u d g e

a human being is not

the centre of the universe

even a wish to help

may create a mass

if you really want

to help

make

commitments

goodness

is a

stage

of

consciousness

recognize

you are yourself

the cause

of the problem

you may have caused

s t e p

o u t

o f

s u f f e r i n g

I AM

is

telling

you

you are

free